Sliders and Rollers

Mini burgers and hot dogs

DAVID COWIE

Sliders and Rollers

Mini burgers and hot dogs

NEW HOLLAND

DAVID COWIE

contents

introduction

The first time I tried a slider I was in West Hollywood, with my wife and some friends. We'd stopped at a hotel for a drink and noticed everyone around us was eating little hamburgers. They looked amazing, so we had to try them as well. What a delicious discovery. Ever since that experience, I've been hooked on these mini burgers—known as sliders—and when I see them on any menu I have to order them to see how they look and how good they taste.

After becoming hooked on sliders, the next thing I had to try was mini hot dogs or, as I like to call them, rollers. Rollers have all your usual hot dog fillings, but are only half the size. And once you've learned how to spiral-cut your sausages, you'll never want to eat a regular dog again.

Sliders and rollers are great snacks. Because of their smaller size, you can serve a selection of meat, seafood and vegetarian sliders and rollers for everyone to sample. Dish them up with some of the tasty sides listed in the Sauces and Sides chapter. And liven up any of the recipes with a homemade sauce—like sauce with a little kick, try Chinese Hot Mustard, want something tangy, try Coriander Yoghurt. These mini burgers and hot dogs make the perfect finger food when friends drop by, whether it's for a backyard barbecue or a fancy cocktail party..

And these little meals can become a part of the everyday family meal: they don't have to be unhealthy. Use lean mince or meat that's been trimmed of fat to make your patties, add plenty of fresh salad fillings and make some low-fat dressings. Put everything into a wholemeal or wholegrain bun and voila, you have healthy sliders and rollers.

Be as creative as you want and make these slider and roller recipes your own. I hope you enjoy eating these delicious treats as much as you enjoy making them.

buns and rolls

THE BUNS and ROLLS

So what is a slider bun? Slider buns are your usual burger buns, just smaller. You can bake them yourself, if you're keen. I'm no baking expert, but I found that after a few attempts I started to get the hang of it and with a little passion and a little patience, I was able to create the perfect small slider bun and hot dog roll.

If you are time-poor or don't want to go to that much trouble, have a look for slider buns at your local supermarket or bakery. You should be able to find small dinner rolls or brioche buns that can be easily used as slider buns. And dinner rolls or mini hot dog rolls are great for rollers. Want to serve sliders and rollers at your next big party? Your local bakery may make some up for you if you order a few dozen rolls or buns.

A trick I sometimes use when I'm time-poor, is to use a cookie cutter to cut out bread buns from larger pieces of bread. I'll buy some flat burger buns and cut out two or three buns from that bread. Or I buy a long loaf of focaccia, Turkish/pide bread or sourdough bread and cut burger buns out of that, using the cookie cutter. You can create a few different varieties of bread buns this way, which is great if you want to serve a selection of sliders at an event.

Brioche-style Buns

1/3 cup lukewarm milk
3 eggs
2 egg yolks
3/4 cup butter, softened
3 1/3 cups all-purpose/plain flour
1/2 cup white sugar
I teaspoon active dry yeast (I packet)

GLAZE
I egg white
2 tablespoons water
1/4 cup of black and white sesame seeds (or just white)

Preheat the oven to 350°F/180°C.

Place the bread ingredients into a bread machine in the order suggested by your manufacturer. Select a dough cycle.

Turn finished dough out onto a lightly floured board and knead for 2–3 minutes. Place in a greased bowl, cover with cling wrap and let rise for 1 hour. The dough should double in size.

Punch down the dough and separate into 15–24 balls/buns. Place onto a baking parchment/paper-lined baking tray with about 3/4 in/2 cm between each bun. Cover with cling wrap and set aside to rise in a warm place until doubled in size.

Whisk together 1 egg white and the water. Brush onto the top of the buns. Sprinkle with black and white sesame seeds.

Bake in the preheated oven until golden brown, about 15–18 minutes.

These French-style bread buns are great with any burger but is a must-have with the Wagyu Beef on a Brioche Bun. After making these buns you will never want to make anything but brioche buns for your sliders.

crusty soft buns

1–2 tablespoons butter, melted
1 egg
1 cup milk
12 oz/520 g all-purpose/plain flour
1 teaspoon salt
1 teaspoon active dried yeast (1 packet)

GLAZE
1 tablespoon butter, melted, or 1 egg white
¼ cup water
¼ cup sesame seeds

In a bowl, whisk together the melted butter, egg and milk. Place the flour, salt and yeast and the egg milk mixture in the bread maker. Select a cycle as per your machine manufacturer's instructions. Run the mix cycle.

When the cycle has finished the mixing, turn out the dough onto a lightly floured surface. Roll the dough to ½ in/1–1.5 cm thickness. Using a 2 in/5 cm cookie cutter cut circles in the dough, cutting the dough close together to get as many buns as possible. Roll the scraps together and let rest for 10–15 minutes then roll and cut again.

Lay the buns out on a baking tray covered with baking parchment/paper, spacing the buns about ¾ in/2 cm apart. Cover the buns with a tea towel and let rise until double in size, about 40 minutes. They will not rise that high but we don't want the rolls to be tall like dinner rolls. Preheat the oven to 375°F/190°C.

Brush the buns with butter to give a soft, light golden crust or the egg water mix to give a shiny dark crust and sprinkle with the sesame seeds. Bake for 12 to 18 minutes until golden brown. Cool the buns on a rack.

Note: Rise time is only a guide as many factors are in play, such as how you kneaded the dough, what yeast you used, so the dough may not double in size during the amount of time indicated. Another way to make the buns, if you don't have a cookie cutter, is to roll the dough into a 2 in/5 cm log and slice the log into ½ in/1–1.5 cm discs and gently shape the buns.

These buns can be turned into slider or roller buns. Use the pizza dough setting on bread maker to mix your dough but don't bake.

Hamburger buns (gluten-free)

2 tablespoons gelatine

2 teaspoons sugar

2 teaspoons salt

1 lb/500g Superfine Flour Mix (see recipe)

2 tablespoons dried yeast

3 egg whites

½ teaspoon citric acid

½ cup olive oil

GLAZE

1 tablespoon butter, melted, or 1 egg white

¼ cup water

¼ cup sesame seeds

Preheat the oven to 400°F/200°C. Grease three heavy pudding trays with margarine. Place 2 cups of cold water into a large mixing bowl and add the gelatine, sugar and salt. Stand for 2 minutes to soften the gelatine. Heat the gelatine mixture for approximately 1 minute until clear. Add the flour and yeast to the warm liquid and beat with an electric mixer for about 1 minute.

Cover the bowl with a large plastic bag. Leave to rise for 10 minutes. Whisk the egg whites and citric acid in a separate bowl until stiff. Add the beaten egg whites and oil to the bread mixture and beat for about 2 minutes.

Separate into 12–16 balls/buns. Place onto a baking tray lined with baking parchment/paper with about ¾ in/2 cm between each bun. Cover with cling wrap and set aside to rise in a warm place until doubled in size. Brush the buns with butter to give a soft, light golden crust or the egg water mix for a shiny dark crust. Bake for 12 to 18 minutes until golden brown. Cool the buns on a rack.

Weigh the ingredients, place them in a large plastic bag and shake well. Sieve into another bag and shake again.

Breakfast Sliders

8 eggs
salt and pepper, to taste
1 tablespoon butter
12 rashers bacon

12 small hash browns
barbecue sauce, to serve
12 wholemeal slider buns

In a bowl, beat the eggs and ¼ cup cold water until combined. Season with salt and pepper.

In a medium non-stick frying pan, heat the butter over a medium-high heat. Once the butter is foaming, add the beaten eggs. Tilt the frying pan to cover the entire frying pan, using a spatula to drag the cooked egg from the outside to the middle of the pan. The omelette should be about ¾ in/2 cm thick. Place the pan under a broiler or grill on medium-high to brown the top of the omelette lightly. Remove from pan and lay flat on a plate or chopping board.

Cut the bacon slices to fit the buns and cook in a frying pan or under the grill until crispy. Bake the hash browns as per the packet instructions. Using a cookie cutter cut out the cooked omelette to fit the buns.

Slice the buns in half lengthways.

To assemble your sliders, add a circle of omelette, a piece of cooked bacon, some barbecue sauce, then a hash brown on top of the bun. Hold it together with a cocktail stick.

The Classic Beef Hamburger With Cheese

1 tablespoon butter

1 small onion, finely diced

1 clove garlic, minced

17½ oz/500 g best-quality ground/minced beef you can afford

1 egg

1 teaspoon Dijon mustard

1 teaspoon Worcestershire sauce

salt and pepper

1 tablespoon olive oil

iceberg lettuce, sliced

3–4 slices cheese (Swiss or Tasty)

2 tomatoes, sliced

pickles

whole egg mayonnaise

12 slider buns of your choice

In a non-stick frying pan on a medium heat melt the butter and cook the onion and garlic until golden and allow to cool.

Place meat in a large bowl and mix in the cooked onion, garlic, egg and Worcestershire sauce, and season with salt and pepper.

Roll into small balls and flatten the patties to fit your buns. Heat the oil in a frying pan and cook for 2–3 minutes until firm to the touch or cooked to your liking.

Slice the buns in half lengthways.

Spread the bottom halves of the buns with mayonnaise, add some lettuce, a cooked patty, a slice of cheese, tomato and cucumber and the top of the bun. Hold the buns together with cocktail sticks and serve while hot.

Serve with tomato or barbecue sauce and pickles on the side.

Double cheeseburger

17½ oz/500 g best-quality ground/minced beef
  you can afford
1 tablespoon butter
1 small brown onion, finely diced
1 clove garlic, minced
1 egg
1 teaspoon Worcestershire sauce

salt and pepper
1 tablespoon olive oil
cheese (Swiss or Tasty, cut each slice into 4 pieces)
hamburger or dill pickles, sliced
your choice of condiments
12 slider buns of your choice

Finely dice the onion and garlic, sweat in butter until golden and allow to cool. Place mince in a large bowl combine with onion, garlic, egg and Worcestershire sauce and season to taste.

Roll into small balls and flatten the patties to fit your buns. Heat the oil and cook the patties for 2–3 minutes for well done or until cooked to your liking.

Remove the patties from the pan and place onto a plate. Add a slice of cheese then another patty then another slice of cheese and leave for the cheese to melt.

Slice your buns in half lengthways.

Add the cooked double cheeseburger patty, top with a slice or two of pickles and your choice of condiments. Put the top bun on and hold the sliders together with a cocktail stick.

Serve this with some classic Beer-battered Fries or The Best Potato Salad.

Serve them while they're hot!

Chilli Cheeseburger

I tablespoon butter
I small brown onion, finely diced
I clove garlic, minced
17½ oz/500 g best-quality ground/minced beef
  you can afford
I egg
I teaspoon Worcestershire sauce
salt and pepper

I tablespoon olive oil
3–4 slices cheese (Swiss or Tasty), cut into
  4 pieces
12 slider buns of your choice
bottled chillies, such as pickled jalapenos or
  chipotle in adobo sauce, diced
hot sauce, such as Tabasco or sriracha sauce
  (a Thai-style hot sauce)

Melt the butter in a non-stick frying pan until bubbling. Sweat the onions and garlic in the frying pan until golden. Allow to cool.

Place mince in a large bowl and combine with the cooked onion, garlic, egg and Worcestershire sauce, and season to taste.

Roll into small balls and flatten the patties to fit your buns. Heat the oil in the frying pan and cook the patties for 2–3 minutes each side, or to your liking.

Set patties aside on a plate and cover each one with a slice of cheese.

Slice the buns in half lengthways and toast them if you like.

To assemble the sliders, add a cooked patty to the bottom half of the buns, add a teaspoon of diced chilli (or more if you like it hot) then add some hot sauce if you want an even hotter kick. Hold them together with a cocktail stick and serve them while hot.

Serve with Oven-baked Onion Rings or South American Bean Salad.

Wagyu Beef Brioche Slider

1 tablespoon butter
1 small brown onion, finely diced
1 clove garlic, finely diced
17½ oz/500 g ground/minced Wagyu beef
1 egg
1 teaspoon Worcestershire sauce
salt and pepper

1 tablespoon olive oil
12 brioche buns
whole egg, full-fat mayonnaise, to taste
iceberg lettuce, sliced
cheese (Swiss or Tasty), sliced
tomato, sliced
cucumber, sliced

Melt the butter in a non-stick frying pan until bubbling. Add the onion and garlic and sweat them until golden. Allow to cool.

Place the mince in a large bowl and combine with the onion, garlic, egg and Worcestershire sauce and season with salt and pepper.

Roll into small balls and flatten the patties to fit your buns. Heat the oil and cook the burgers for 2–3 minutes each side until firm to the touch or cooked to your liking.

Cut your buns in half lengthways. Spread the mayonnaise on the bottom half of the buns. Add some lettuce, a cooked patty then add the sliced cheese so it melts with heat of the slider, then tomato, cucumber and the top of the bun. Hold the buns together with cocktail sticks and serve them hot.

Serve with a side of Beer-battered Fries.

beef sliders

1 tablespoon butter

1 small onion, finely diced

1 clove garlic, minced

17½ oz/500 g best-quality ground/minced beef you can afford

1 egg

1 teaspoon Dijon mustard

1 teaspoon Worcestershire sauce

salt and pepper

1 tablespoon olive oil

iceberg lettuce, sliced

spanish onion, finely sliced

1–2 tomatoes, sliced

pickles, to serve

In a non-stick frying pan on a medium heat melt the butter and cook the onion and garlic until golden and allow to cool.

Place meat in a large bowl and mix in the cooked onion, garlic, egg, Worcestershire sauce and season with salt and pepper.

Roll into small balls and flatten the patties to fit your buns. Heat the oil in a frying pan and cook for about 2–3 minutes until firm to the touch or cooked to your liking.

Slice the buns in half lengthways.

Spread the bottom halves of the buns with tomato sauce. Add on a cooked patty, some lettuce, onion, tomato and the top of the bun. Hold the buns together with cocktail sticks and serve while hot.

Serve with tomato or barbecue sauce and pickles on the side.

Chicken Schnitzel Sliders

1 cup panko breadcrumbs
salt and pepper, to taste
2 eggs
17½ oz/500 g chicken breast fillets, cut into
    pieces to fit buns
1 tablespoon olive oil

whole egg mayonnaise or some Onion Relish
    (see recipe)
2 tomatoes, sliced
1 cup baby spinach
12 slider buns of your choice

In a shallow bowl, combine the panko breadcrumbs, salt and pepper.

In another bowl, beat the two eggs. Dip the chicken pieces in the beaten egg, shake off excess then dip into the panko breadcrumbs.

In a non-stick frying pan, heat the oil on a medium-high heat and cook the schnitzels until golden brown for 4–5 minutes each side.

Slice your buns in half lengthwise and toast.

To assemble your sliders, spread on the mayonnaise on the bottom half of the buns, add a piece of schnitzel, a slice or two of tomato, some spinach leaves and the top of the bun. Hold together with cocktail stick.

Add a slice of crispy bacon if you want and serve with the Baby Spinach, Toasted Pine Nut and Avocado Salad.

Sliders and rollers are great food for parties—serve them on large platters so people can grab them while they mingle. They won't last long!

chicken and bacon club slider

17½ oz/500 g ground/minced chicken
½ cup dried breadcrumbs
1 tablespoon milk
2 scallions/spring onions, finely sliced
2 tablespoons parsley, finely chopped
salt and pepper, to taste
1 tablespoon olive oil

12 rashes shortcut bacon
12 slider buns of your choice
whole egg mayonnaise, to serve
½ cos lettuce
4 roma tomatoes, sliced

Place ground chicken, breadcrumbs and milk in a large bowl. Mix in the scallions and parsley, and season to taste.

Roll into small balls and flatten the sliders to fit your buns. Heat the oil in the frying pan and cook the patties for 2–3 minutes each side or to your liking at the same time that you cook the bacon.

Slice the buns in half lengthwise and toast them. To assemble the sliders, spread the mayonnaise on the bottom half of the buns, add some lettuce, a patty, then top with a slice or two of tomato, a slice of bacon and the top of the bun. Hold it all together with a cocktail stick.

Serve with Spicy Baked Wedges and Sour Cream. Instead of whole egg mayo, why not try these with some Blue Cheese Mayonnaise.

Greek Lamb sliders

17½ oz/500 g ground/minced lamb
1 small onion, finely diced
1 clove garlic, minced
1 teaspoon ground cumin
1 teaspoon ground coriander
1 egg
1 teaspoon chilli flakes (optional)

salt and pepper, to taste
1 tablespoon olive oil
1 Lebanese cucumber, finely sliced with vegetable peeler
Tzatziki or Garlic Mayonnaise (see recipe)
salt and pepper, to taste
2 turkish pide loaves, cut into 12 rings

Using a cookie cutter, cut out rounds from the bread to create your slider buns.

Place mince in a large bowl and mix together with the onion, garlic, cumin, coriander, egg, chilli flakes, if using, and season with salt and pepper.

Roll into small balls and flatten the patties to fit your buns. Heat the oil in a non-stick frying pan and cook for 3–4 minutes each side or to your liking.

To assemble your sliders, add some lettuce to the bun, a cooked patty then a slice or two of tomato and cucumber. Finally, add a dollop of tzatziki. Place the bun on top and hold everything together with a cocktail stick. Serve them while hot.

These sliders are great with the Tomato and Onion Salad with Feta Dressing or the Greek Salad.

TURKEY SLIDERS

2 tablespoons olive oil
1 small onion, finely diced
1 clove garlic, minced
17½ oz/500 g turkey
1 teaspoon Worcestershire sauce
salt and pepper, to taste
4–6 cheese slices (Swiss or Tasty), cut in half

12 strips streaky bacon
12 slider buns of your choice
mayonnaise
seeded or Dijon mustard
12 slider buns of your choice

Heat a tablespoon of oil in a frying pan on a medium heat. Cook the onion and garlic in the pan until golden and allow to cool.

Place the turkey in a large bowl and add the cooked onion and garlic, Worcestershire sauce and season with salt and pepper. Mix together until well-combined.

Roll into small balls and flatten the patties to fit your buns. In a non-stick frying pan heat the rest of the oil and cook the patties for 3–4 minutes each side until brown. Place a slice of cheese on top of each patty for the last minute of cooking. While the patties are cooking, cook the bacon in another pan until crispy.

Slice the buns in half lengthwise. Spread the bottom half of the buns with mayonnaise, add a cooked turkey patty with the melted cheese, a slice of bacon and a dollop of mustard on top. Add the top of the bun and hold it together with a cocktail stick. Serve while hot.

Try these with some Oven-baked Potato Fries.

Cajun Chicken, avocado and bacon Ciabatta Sliders

17½ oz/500 g skinless chicken thighs
1 tablespoon cumin
1 tablespoon ground coriander
1 tablespoon hot or mild paprika
salt and pepper, to taste
2 tablespoons olive oil

6 bacon rashers
mayonnaise, to serve
2 avocados, sliced
1 cup arugula/rocket
12 ciabatta slider buns

Cut the chicken thighs into pieces to fit the slider bun. In a bowl, combine the cumin, ground coriander, paprika, salt and pepper.

In a shallow dish, lay out the chicken and drizzle with 1 tablespoon of oil then sprinkle the spices over the chicken and rub in well.

In a large, non-stick frying pan heat the remaining oil on a medium-high heat and cook the chicken for 4–5 minutes each side until firm. While the chicken is cooking, fry the bacon in another non-stick frying pan until crispy.

Slice the buns in half lengthwise and toast them.

To assemble the sliders, dollop the bottom buns with mayonnaise, spread on some arugula, a piece of chicken, sliced avocado and top with bacon. Place on the top bun and hold the slider together with a cocktail stick.

pork belly sliders with spicy caramel sauce

2 lb 4 oz/1 kg boneless pork belly
1 cup water
½ cup sugar
1–2 long red chillies, de-seeded
1 teaspoon fish sauce

1 tablespoon soy sauce
juice of half a lime
½ cup fresh cilantro/coriander
salt and pepper to taste
12 brioche buns

Preheat the oven at 420°F/220°C.

Score the pork belly skin at ½ in/1 cm intervals in squares the same size as the buns. Place the pork on a rack in a roasting pan, skin-side up. Pat dry the pork belly with paper towel and rub salt into the skin. Pour water into the roasting pan, enough to fill the pan to just under the rack. Place in the oven and roast for 30 minutes or until the skin is crispy. Reduce the heat to 350°F/180°C and roast for a further 1½ hours or until the meat is tender, topping up with water as necessary. Remove the pork and cut into squares to fit the buns, as scored before cooking.

In a saucepan, bring the water and sugar to the boil. Boil until it starts to caramelise. Add the chillies, fish sauce and the soy. Reduce the heat and simmer until the liquid has reduced by half, squeeze in the lime juice then set aside for later use.

Slice the buns in half lengthways.

To assemble the sliders, add a piece of pork and drizzle over with some caramel dressing. Top with a few cilantro leaves then the top bun. Hold together with a cocktail stick.

Serve with Asian-style Coleslaw on the side.

Chinese-style Barbecued Pork Sliders

2 tablespoons hoisin sauce (Chinese barbecue sauce)

3 tablespoons dark soy sauce

2 tablespoons shaoxing wine or dry cooking sherry

salt, to taste

¼ teaspoon Chinese five spice

1 teaspoon chilli flakes (optional)

¼ cup brown sugar

1 teaspoon red food colouring (optional)

2–3 pork (tenderloins) fillets

12 slider buns of your choice

1 cos lettuce (or any lettuce you prefer), torn

2–3 tomatoes, thinly sliced

Chinese Hot Mustard (see recipe)

char siu sauce, to serve

plum sauce, to serve

12 slider buns of your choice

Mix the hoisin, soy, wine, salt, five spice, chilli flakes, sugar and red food dye in a shallow dish big enough to lay your fillets in.

Place the fillets in the dish and turn the fillets to coat. Cover with cling wrap and refrigerate overnight if possible or at least two hours.

Preheat the oven to 350°F/180°C. Using a roasting tray with a rack, fill the tray with about ½ in/1 cm water or enough to come below the rack level. Place the fillets on the rack and put the tray in the oven, cooking for 40 minutes, turning after 20 minutes. Brush the fillets occasionally while they are cooking with the leftover marinade. Remove and cool, before slicing thinly.

Slice the burger buns in half lengthwise and toast them. Add some lettuce to the bottom half of the buns, add a piece or two of pork to each bun. Top the pork with mustard, char siu or plum sauce and add a slice of tomato. Hold the sliders together with cocktail sticks and serve hot or cold.

A side of Asian-style Coleslaw would be delicious with this slider.

candied bacon BLT sliders

12 slices thick-cut bacon
½ cup brown sugar
I teaspoon chilli flakes
I teaspoon ground pepper

mayonnaise
lettuce, sliced
2 tomatoes, sliced
12 slider buns of your choice

Preheat the oven to 300°F/150°C. Line a baking tray with foil.

Arrange the bacon strips in a single layer on the baking tray. Combine the brown sugar, chilli flakes and pepper in small bowl. Rub sugar mixture over both sides of the bacon strips and bake until crisp, 30 to 40 minutes, turning the bacon over halfway through the cooking.

When the bacon is crispy and sticky remove from oven and cut into pieces to fit buns then set aside to cool.

Slice the slider buns in half lengthways. Toast the buns and spread mayonnaise on top and bottom bun.

To assemble your sliders, add the lettuce to the bottom bun, add a few slices of candied bacon, some tomato slices, then the top bun. Hold together with a cocktail stick.

Serve with Warm Herbed Potato Salad.

Ham and pineapple sliders

4–5 ham steaks
1 x 9 oz/250 g can pineapple pieces
12 slices cheddar cheese, cut to fit the ham steak

1 teaspoon olive oil
tomato or barbecue sauce, to serve
12 slider buns of your choice

Cut your ham steaks into rounds or squares to fit your slider buns.

In a frying pan, heat the oil on a medium-high heat and cook the ham steaks, turning until golden, about 3–4 minutes.

Slice the buns in half lengthwise and toast the bun bottoms. Place a ham steak, add a slice of cheese and top with some pineapple. Place the bottom buns under the griller or broiler until the cheese melts. Toast the top buns as well. Once the cheese has melted place the tops on the buns and thread a cocktail stick through the middle of the sliders, to hold them together. Serve with tomato or barbecue sauce. If you like, use sweet chilli sauce instead.

Try this with a side of Pineapple Salsa or South American Bean Salad.

Meatloaf Sliders

9 oz/250 g ground/minced beef
9 oz/250 g ground/minced pork
9 oz/250 g ground/minced lamb
¾ cup dried breadcrumbs
I large white onion, diced
I large egg
¼ cup tomato paste
I teaspoon Worcestershire sauce
2 cloves garlic, minced

I teaspoon chilli powder
I teaspoon ground cumin
salt and pepper to taste
½ cup barbecue sauce
7oz/200 g Swiss or Tasty cheese, grated
mayonnaise or Onion Chutney (see recipe), to
  serve
12 slider buns of your choice

In a large bowl, combine the meats, breadcrumbs, onion, egg, tomato paste, Worcestershire sauce, garlic and spices.

Shape into a loaf to fit the size of the buns on a baking tray covered with baking parchment/paper. You may need to make more than one loaf. Bake the meat loaf at 350°F/180°C for 35 minutes, brushing with the barbecue sauce at 25 minutes. Remove and rest for 10 minutes before slicing. Slice meatloaf thickly and serve hot or cold.

Slice the buns in half lengthways.

To assemble your sliders, add a slice of meatloaf, drizzle over some barbecue sauce and sprinkle with some grated cheese. Place on the top of the bun. Hold together with a cocktail stick.

Serve with Sweet Coleslaw.

popcorn shrimp sliders

½ cup cornstarch/cornflour
I cup panko breadcrumbs
salt and pepper
2 eggs
24 medium to large shrimp/prawns, peeled and
   de-veined

I ½ cups vegetable oil, for deep-frying
½ small lettuce, shredded
¼ cup Wasabi Mayonnaise (see recipe)
12 slider buns of your choice

Place the cornstarch into a wide, shallow dish and season with salt and peper. Place the breadcrumbs in a separate shallow dish.

In a bowl, beat the eggs with two teaspoons of water. Dredge shrimp in the seasoned flour. Dip the shrimp into the egg mixture, then into the breadcrumbs.

Heat the oil in a pan at a medium heat then deep-fry the shrimp in batches until they are crispy and golden. Drain them on kitchen paper.

Slice the buns in half lengthways.

To assemble your sliders, add the lettuce to the bottom halves of the buns and top with one or two popcorn shrimp, depending on the size. Spoon on some Wasabi Mayonnaise then the top of the bun. Hold the bun together with a cocktail stick.

These sliders are fantastic with Beer-battered Fries and Tartare Sauce.

Why not let your friends make their own? Set up a table with a selection of buns and rolls, patties and fillings. Assemble a variety of condiments to suit everyone's taste. Then just let your guests help themselves! Don't forget to have some cocktail sticks handy so everyone can keep their sliders together.

Bacon-wrapped scallop sliders

6 slices streaky bacon, cut in half lengthwise
12 large scallops, roe off (U15 size)
spray oil
1 lemon

12 small brioche buns
Spicy Seafood Sauce (see recipe), to serve

Preheat the oven to 350°F/180°C. Line a baking tray with baking parchment/paper and lay out the bacon in a single layer.

Bake until the bacon is just golden but still soft and pliable, about 10 minutes. Remove and cool on some paper towel to remove excess oil.

Wrap a slice of bacon around each scallop and secure it with a toothpick. Place on the baking tray lined with baking parchment/paper, season with salt and pepper and squeeze lemon juice all over. Return the tray to the oven and bake for 12–15 minutes or until the bacon is sizzling and crispy.

Slice the brioche buns in half. To assemble your sliders, remove the toothpicks from the scallop, place on a bun, add some spicy seafood sauce and add the top bun. Push a cocktail stick through the slider, to hold it together, and serve.

cajun-style crumbed Fish Sliders

I cup breadcrumbs

2 tablespoons Cajun seasoning

I cup all-purpose/plain flour

salt and pepper to taste

2 eggs

17½ oz/500 g firm, white fish (snapper would be good), cut into pieces to fit the buns

I teaspoon olive oil

12 slider buns of your choice

mixed salad leaves

3 roma tomatoes, sliced

red/Spanish onion, finely sliced

12 wholemeal slider buns

Garlic Mayonnaise (see recipe), to serve

In a shallow bowl, combine the breadcrumbs and Cajun seasoning. In another shallow bowl, mix together the flour, salt and pepper.

In a bowl, beat the two eggs. Toss the fish pieces in the flour and shake off any excess then coat the fish in the egg then the breadcrumbs.

In a non-stick frying pan, heat the oil on a medium–high heat and cook the fish until golden brown, about 3–4 minutes.

To assemble your sliders, cut the buns in half. Add some salad leaves, sliced tomato, onion and a piece of cooked fish. Dollop on some mayonnaise and place the bun on the top. Pierce a cocktail stick through the burger to hold it all together and serve while they are hot.

Top with sweet chilli sauce or use Turkish pide bread instead of slider buns—just cut rounds out of the pide bread with a cookie cutter.

Tuna Sliders

1 x 15 oz/425 g tinned tuna in brine, drained
½ cup dried breadcrumbs
½ white onion, diced
2 tablespoons fresh parsley, finely chopped
2 teaspoons Dijon mustard
¼ cup mayonnaise
juice of half a lemon
1 teaspoon hot sauce (Tabasco or sriracha)

1 egg
1 tablespoon olive oil
salt and pepper, to taste
1 cup mixed salad leaves, torn
3–4 tomatoes, sliced
Tartare Sauce (see recipe), to serve
12 slider buns of your choice

Combine the tuna, breadcrumbs, onion, parsley, mustard, mayonnaise, lemon juice, hot sauce and egg in a large bowl and mix until well combined.

Roll into small balls and flatten the patties to fit your buns. Heat the oil in a large frying pan over a medium heat. Cook the patties until brown, about 3–4 minutes each side and set aside on some kitchen towel to drain.

To assemble your sliders, slice your buns in half. Add some mixed salad leaves, a slice or two of tomato and the tuna patty. Dollop with some tartare sauce and add the top of the bun. Use a cocktail stick to hold the burger together. Serve them hot.

You could also serve this with sweet chilli sauce instead of tartare, if you want some extra heat.

These are so quick and easy to make, you'll be whipping up a batch every time someone drops in for a beer.

crab cake sliders

17½ oz/500 g cooked crab meat
9 oz/250 g mashed potato
2 scallions/spring onions, chopped
1 tablespoon parsley, finely chopped
1 egg
½ teaspoon onion salt
pepper, to taste

1 cup panko breadcrumbs (use regular
  breadcrumbs if you can't get panko)
2 tablespoons olive oil
12 slider buns of your choice
1 quantity Tartare Sauce (see recipe) or sweet
  chilli sauce

In a large bowl, combine the crab meat, mashed potato, onion, parsley and egg then season with salt and pepper. Chill the mixture in the refrigerator for an hour. Then form patties to fit your rolls and roll in panko breadcrumbs, pressing the patties in well.

Heat oil in a frying pan over medium heat until hot. Fry the patties until golden brown in batches and drain on paper towel. Keep warm in a low oven until ready to assemble sliders.

To assemble your sliders, cut the buns in half. Add some lettuce and a patty to a bun then dollop on some tartare sauce or sweet chilli sauce. Add the top of the bun. Use a cocktail stick to hold the burger together until serving.

Serve with Tartare Sauce or Sweet Chilli Yoghurt.

crumbed fish sliders

1 cup dried breadcrumbs
1 cup all-purpose/plain flour
salt and pepper, to taste
2 eggs
17½ oz/500 g firm white-flesh fish (snapper), cut
   into pieces to fit the buns
1 teaspoon olive oil

mayonnaise to serve
lettuce leaves
1–2 roma tomatoes, sliced
1 red/Spanish onion, finely sliced
12 slider buns of your choice

Pour the breadcrumbs into a shallow bowl. Pour the flour into another shallow bowl and season it with salt and pepper.

In a bowl, beat the two eggs. Toss the fish pieces in the flour and shake off any excess. Dip into the egg then the breadcrumbs.

In a non-stick frying pan, heat the oil on a medium-high heat and cook the fish until golden brown, about 3–4 minutes.

To assemble your sliders, cut the buns, spread on the mayonnaise. Add some lettuce, a fish fillet, tomato slice and onion. Place the bun on top and thread a cocktail stick through the burger to hold it together and serve.

Serve with Tomato Chilli Jam Salsa or Spicy Seafood Sauce.

Pumpkin and Cilantro Sliders

6 cups grated pumpkin
2 eggs
2 onions, finely chopped
1 bunch cilantro/coriander, finely chopped leaves
  and roots
½ cup all-purpose/plain flour
1 teaspoon ground cumin seeds
salt and pepper to taste

breadcrumbs
olive oil for frying
12 slider buns of your choice
2 cups salad leaves, for serving
2 tomatoes, sliced
1 red/Spanish onion, sliced into rings
seeded mustard, to serve

Place the pumpkin, eggs, onions, cilantro, flour, cumin and salt and pepper in a large bowl and mix to combine.

Roll heaped tablespoons of mixture into the dry breadcrumbs and form into small patties. Place patties on a plate or tray and refrigerate for 30 minutes.

Heat a frying pan on high, add 2 tablespoons of olive oil and reduce heat to medium.

Fry the patties for about 4 minutes each side until crisp and golden brown. Set aside on some paper towel to drain.

Slice the buns in half. To assemble the sliders, add a lettuce leaf or two, to each burger half. Add on the cooked patty, some sliced tomato and onion rings. Drizzle some seeded mustard onto the other slider bun and place it on top. Hold the slider together with a cocktail stick.

Spice up the patties with the addition of chilli flakes or add some Sweet Chilli Yoghurt sauce. Serve with Barley, Feta and Pear Salad.

Rice and vegetable sliders

¼ cup brown rice, cooked
¾ cup oat flour
1 small onion, finely diced
1 clove garlic, crushed
1 in/2 cm piece fresh ginger, grated
4 oz/120 g canned sweetcorn, drained
½ carrot, grated
1 small zucchini/courgettes grated
2 tablespoons pine nuts, toasted
1 tablespoon peanut butter

1 teaspoon soy sauce
1½ tablespoons natural yoghurt
1 egg white
1¼ cup dried breadcrumbs
1 tablespoon olive oil
12 slider buns of your choice
mixed salad leaves
sweet chilli sauce, to serve
1 lemon, quartered, to serve

Place rice, flour, onion, garlic, ginger, sweetcorn, carrot, zucchini and pine nuts in a bowl and mix to combine. Place peanut butter, soy sauce, yoghurt and egg white in a food processor and process to combine. Add peanut butter mixture and ½ cup breadcrumbs to rice mixture and mix well.

Shape the rice mixture into 12 patties and coat with the remaining breadcrumbs. Heat the oil in a non-stick frying pan and cook patties for 5 minutes each side or until golden and cooked through. Drain on absorbent kitchen paper.

Slice the buns in half. To assemble the sliders, add some mixed salad leaves to the bottom bun, then the patty and drizzle with sweet chilli sauce. Hold together with a cocktail stick. Serve with lemon wedges.

Wild Rice and Bean Sliders

30 oz/880 g canned soybeans, drained and rinsed

2 cup fresh cilantro/coriander, chopped

2 scallions/spring onions, chopped

1 in/2 cm piece fresh ginger, finely grated

2 tablespoon ground cumin

2 tablespoon ground coriander

1 teaspoon ground turmeric

1 cup wild rice, cooked

1 cup wholemeal flour

2 eggs, lightly beaten

4 tablespoons vegetable oil

12 slider buns of your choice

mixed salad leaves, to serve

Sweet Chilli Yoghurt (see recipe)

Preheat barbecue to a medium heat. Place soybeans, fresh cilantro, scallions, ginger, cumin, ground coriander and turmeric into a food processor and process for 30 seconds or until mixture resembles coarse breadcrumbs. Transfer mixture to a bowl, add rice, flour and egg, and mix to combine. Shape mixture into 12 patties.

Heat oil on barbecue plate for 2–3 minutes or until hot, add patties and cook for 5 minutes each side or until golden and heated through.

Slice buns in half.

To assemble the sliders, place mixed leaves, the patty and a spoonful of sweet chilli yoghurt, on the bottom half of each roll, top with remaining roll half and serve immediately. Hold together with a cocktail stick.

vegetable sliders

14 oz/400 g broccoli, chopped
14 oz/400 g zucchini/courgette, chopped
7 oz/200 g carrots, chopped
1 onion, finely chopped
2 cloves garlic, crushed
¼ cup parsley, chopped

3 cups dried breadcrumbs
½ cup all-purpose/plain flour, sifted
black pepper
½ cos lettuce leaves
Spicy Tomato Sauce (see recipe)
12 slider buns of your choice

To make patties, boil, steam or microwave broccoli, zucchini and carrots until tender. Drain, rinse under cold running water and pat dry.

Place broccoli, zucchini, carrots, onions, garlic and parsley in a food processor and process until puréed. Transfer vegetable mixture to a mixing bowl, add breadcrumbs and flour, season with black pepper and mix to combine. Cover and refrigerate for 30 minutes.

Shape mixture into 12 patties. Place on a tray lined with non-stick baking parchment/paper, cover and refrigerate until required.

Preheat barbecue to a medium heat. Cook patties on a lightly oiled barbecue plate for 3–4 minutes each side. Slice 12 slider buns in half and toast buns on barbecue. To assemble the sliders, place a leaf of lettuce on each bun, then the patty and a spoonful of Spicy Tomato Sauce, on the bottom half of each roll, top with remaining roll half and serve immediately. Hold together with a cocktail stick.

crusty herbed lentil sliders

1 x 15 oz/440 g can brown lentils

1 large white onion, finely chopped

1 tablespoon olive oil

4 large garlic cloves, peeled

1¾ oz/50 g parmesan cheese, grated

½ cup dill, parsley or cilantro/coriander

salt and pepper to taste

3 tablespoons milk or water

1 cup dried breadcrumbs

½ cup grated parmesan cheese, extra

½ cup chives, finely chopped

2 eggs

4 tablespoons oil, for cooking lentil cakes

1 cos lettuce, leaves torn

4 tomatoes, sliced

1 cucumber, sliced

sweet chilli sauce, to serve

12 slider buns of your choice

Drain the lentils.

Chop the onion finely. Heat 1 tablespoon of oil in a frying pan and fry the onion until deep golden brown. Add the garlic to the onions and sauté until golden. Set aside.

Mix the cold lentils, cooked onion/garlic mixture, parmesan cheese, herbs, and salt and pepper to taste, adding the milk or water if necessary, to loosen the mixture. Form the mixture into small cakes. Freeze the lentil cakes for 30 minutes to make them easier to coat. In a large bowl, mix the breadcrumbs, extra parmesan cheese and chives together and set aside.

Beat the eggs in a bowl, then dip each lentil cake into the egg and then into the breadcrumb mixture, pressing the crumbs firmly onto the surface. Chill until ready to cook.

Preheat oven to 285°F/140°C (to keep warm). Heat some oil in a frying pan and cook the lentil cakes in hot oil, over a medium-high heat until they are brown and crispy all over. Transfer the cooked lentil cakes to a preheated oven on a wire rack to keep warm while you cook the other lentil cakes.

Cut the buns in half lengthways. Add some lettuce, a cooked patty then tomato, cucumber and some sweet chilli sauce. Place the top half of the bun on top and hold it together with cocktail sticks. Serve them hot.

Fennel and zucchini Sliders

²/₃ cup all-purpose/plain flour

1 egg, separated

1 tablespoon olive oil

¼ teaspoon salt and freshly ground pepper

1 medium fennel bulb

1 large zucchini/courgette

1 tablespoon mint, chopped

vegetable oil, for shallow frying

12 slider buns of your choice

1–2 tomatoes, sliced

mixed salad leaves, to serve

9 oz/250 g Tzatziki (see recipe), to serve

Sift the flour into a bowl and make a well. Into the well add the egg yolk and mix the flour and egg together until a smooth batter has formed. Season with salt and pepper, cover and leave to thicken for 30 minutes in a cool place.

Grate the fennel and zucchini and stir the chopped mint into the batter. Whisk the egg white until soft peaks form and fold gently into the batter mixture.

Place a heavy-based frying pan over a medium heat and lightly coat with oil. Using a tablespoon, add measured amounts of mixture to the pan, a few at a time. When golden, turn and cook on the other side. Repeat until all the mixture has been used. Drain on absorbent paper.

Slice the slider buns in half. Place a patty on the bottom half of the bun, dollop with Tzatziki, add a slice of tomato, some mixed salad leaves and the top half of the bun. Serve warm.

Felafel Sliders

3 cups canned chickpeas/garbanzo beans, drained
  and rinsed
1 teaspoon ground coriander
1 bunch fresh cilantro/coriander
3 cloves garlic, minced
½ bunch parsley
1 teaspoon ground cumin
¼ teaspoon cayenne pepper
2 teaspoons salt or to taste

black pepper to taste
1½ oz/40 g all-purpose/plain flour
1 cup sesame seeds
1 cup peanut oil, for frying
2 cups mixed salad leaves
Quick Tomato Salsa (see recipe), to serve
hummus or Garlic Mayonnaise (see recipe),
  to serve
12 slider buns of your choice

Drain, rinse and grind the chickpeas in a food processor with the spices, herbs, garlic, salt and pepper and flour, mixing until moist. If the moisture seems too dry, add some water to the mixture as it is processed.

Shape the felafel mixture into balls about 2 in/5 cm across, roll into the sesame seeds. If you want you can leave them round or flatten into patties.

Heat the peanut oil and fry the felafel patties until deep golden brown.

Cut your buns in half lengthways. Add some mixed leaves, some Tomato Salsa, add a dollop of hummus or Garlic Mayonnaise and top with the bun. Hold the buns together with cocktail sticks and serve them hot.

For a change, you could get some pita bread or pide bread and cut out slider buns using cookie cutters.

Emaleigh's Chickpea Veggie Sliders

1 tin chickpeas/garbanzo beans, drained

2 eggs

1 tablespoon olive oil plus extra for frying

1 onion, finely diced

1 clove garlic, minced

1 carrot, very finely diced

2 stalks celery, diced

1–2 zucchini/courgettes, diced

1 teaspoon ground cumin

1 teaspoon ground coriander

salt and pepper to taste

½ cup rolled oats

½ cup dried breadcrumbs

whole egg mayonnaise

lettuce, to serve

Tomato Salsa (see recipe), to serve

12 slider buns of your choice

In a food processor, add the chickpeas and eggs. Pulse the mix to combine but don't over-mix—you don't want a purée.

In a frying pan, heat the oil on a medium heat and add the onion, garlic, carrot and celery. Cook until the vegetables have softened, then add the zucchini and the dried spices. Season to taste and cook for another 2 minutes.

Let the vegetable mixture cool in a large bowl for 5 minutes. Stir in the chickpea and egg mixture until combined, then the oats and breadcrumbs. Let the mixture sit for 10 minutes for the oats and breadcrumbs to soak up the liquid.

Roll the mixture into small balls the size of golf balls, then flatten to form patties.

Heat some oil in a frying pan over a medium heat and cook the patties for 5 minutes or until they are golden brown on each side.

To assemble your sliders, cut the buns, spread on the Tomato Salsa, the lettuce, then the top of the bun. Hold together with a cocktail stick and serve them while hot.

Red lentil sliders

2 cups water
¾ cup dried red lentils
¾ teaspoon salt
1 cup onion, diced
½ cup carrot, finely diced
3 garlic cloves, chopped
2 cups mushrooms, roughly chopped
1 teaspoon dried marjoram
¼ teaspoon black pepper

⅓ cup dried breadcrumbs
1 tablespoon fresh lemon juice
2 egg whites
2 tablespoons vegetable oil
2–3 cups baby spinach leaves
mayonnaise or Tzatziki (see recipe)
red onion, sliced into rings
12 slider buns of your choice

Combine water, lentils, and ¼ teaspoon salt in a medium saucepan and bring to the boil. Cover, reduce heat to medium-low and simmer for 20 minutes. Drain then set aside.

Heat oil in a large non-stick fry pan on medium-high heat. Add the onion, carrot and the garlic cloves and cook until onions are golden brown. Add ½ teaspoon salt, mushrooms, marjoram and pepper.

Cook for 3 minutes, stirring occasionally. Place onion mixture in a large bowl and let stand for 5 minutes. Then add the lentils, breadcrumbs, lemon juice and egg whites and mix together. Cover and place in refrigerator for 30 minutes to help firm the mixture.

Divide the lentil mixture into 12 equal portions, shaping each portion into a 1 cm/½ in thick patty. Heat the vegetable oil in a non-stick fry pan over medium heat. Add lentil patties and cook for 5 minutes on each side.

To assemble your sliders, cut the buns in half, spread one half with tomato salsa, add some spinach, a lentil patty then a spoonful of mayonnaise or Tzatziki. Add the top of the burger bun. Use cocktail sticks to hold the burger together and serve them while they're hot.

Serve this with a fresh salad on the side.

rollers

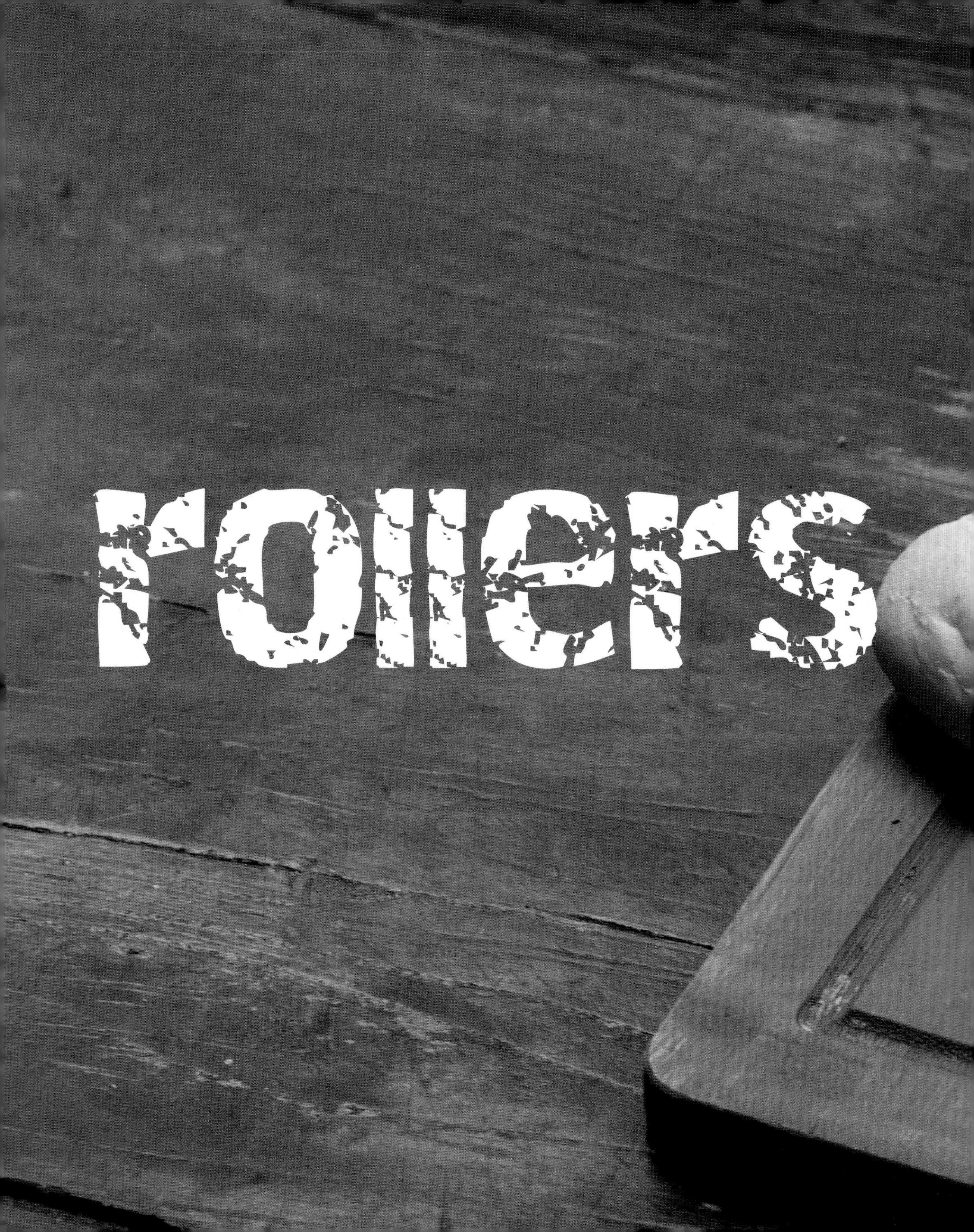

some quick tricks before you get rolling

To make little sausages from normal-size sausages:

Buy linked sausages. In the middle of the first sausage just twist it in half to form two smaller sausages. Give them around 5 or so turns then, with the next sausage, twist the opposite way to form the next two small sausages. If you try with unlinked sausages the ends will come apart.

Continue twisting the sausages this way until you have the number you want to use, then cut the links with a knife.

how to spiral-cut your cocktail franks

To create a spiral-cut hot dog frank, get a long wooden skewer and thread the sausage onto the skewer.

Next, hold one end of the skewer and with a knife in the other hand start cutting into one end of the sausage at approximately 45 degrees. Cut from one end of the sausage to the other, making sure you don't cut all the way through, as you slowly turn the skewer, rolling the frank as you cut.

Pull out the stick and there you have a spiral frank ready for grilling.

You can then fry the sausages on the grill or in a frying pan, or boil in a pot of water. The spiral cut increases the surface area of the sausage and the grooves in the sausage allow your condiments and sauces to completely cover the sausage.

classic hot dog rollers

12 cocktail franks
12 small roller buns (hot dog buns)
1 cup cheddar cheese, grated

mustard, to serve
ketchup, to serve

Cook the franks on a barbecue, grill or boil them. Split the rollers lengthwise and, if you like, toast the buns. Add the cooked franks to the roller bun then top with the cheese.

This roller is so versatile, you can add any of your favourite sauces or mustards.

Spiral-cut Rollers With Chilli

12 cocktail franks (spiral cut to take more chilli)
oil, for frying
12 roller buns of your choice

14 oz/400 g Chilli for Rollers (see recipe)
1 large red/Spanish onion, diced
1 cup cheddar cheese, grated (optional)

Cook the franks on a hot barbecue or frying pan in a little oil, until cooked through.

Cut the roller buns lengthwise. Add the cooked franks to the roller bun. Top with some warm Chilli and onion, then add cheese, if you are using it.

To serve, add mustard or tomato sauce and any of your favourite toppings. These classic hot dogs are great with chips.

spiral-cut rollers with bacon and onion

4 short-cut bacon, thickly diced
1 onion, diced
12 cocktail franks

12 roller buns of your choice
oil, for frying

Fry the diced bacon until crispy. Set aside on some paper towel then, in the same pan, cook the onion until it is golden brown. Spiral-cut the franks and fry them on a hot barbecue or in a frying pan with a little oil.

Cut the roller buns lengthwise. Add the cooked franks to the roller bun, then sprinkle the bacon and diced onion into the spiral cuts.

Add your favourite toppings, sauce or mustard.

Serve with Oven-baked Onion Rings.

spiral-cut rollers with tomato salsa

12 cocktail franks
oil, for frying
1 cup Quick Tomato Salsa (see recipe)

12 roller buns of your choice
mustard

Spiral-cut the franks and barbecue or grill them to your liking in a little oil. Cut the roller buns in half lengthwise and toast the buns if you like. Add the cooked franks to the roller bun then the Tomato Salsa.

Add your favourite sauces, mustard or chilli sauce.

Cutting your sausages with a spiral cut not only looks good but holds more toppings.

Lamb Fillet Rollers

I teaspoon ground cumin
I teaspoon sweet paprika
½ teaspoon cayenne pepper
salt, to taste
I–2 lamb fillets
I tablespoon olive oil

12 roller buns of your choice
3 small tomatoes, thinly sliced
I cup baby spinach leaves
½ cup feta, crumbed
½ cup Tzatziki (see recipe)

In a shallow dish combine cumin, paprika, cayenne pepper and salt to taste. Coat the lamb fillet with the mixed spices.

Heat the oil in large non-stick frying pan and cook for 3–4 minutes each side for medium or to your liking. Remove from the pan and let the meat rest for 4 minutes before slicing the lamb diagonally into ½ in/1 cm slices.

Slice the rollers in half lengthways. Add the tomato, spinach, lamb and some feta. Dollop with some tzatziki sauce before serving.

Serve With Tomato and Onion Salad With Feta Dressing.

Meat Ball Rollers

9 oz/250 g ground/minced pork
9 oz/250 g ground/minced beef
¼ cup fresh breadcrumbs
1 onion, finely diced
1 clove garlic
½ teaspoon oregano
½ teaspoon parsley

½ teaspoon dry chilli flakes (optional)
1 egg
salt and pepper to taste
Tomato Sauce for Meatballs (see recipe)
18–20 roller buns of your choice
7 oz/200 g provolone cheese, sliced
extra cheese, to serve

Preheat the oven to 350°F/180°C. Line a baking tray with baking parchment/paper.

In a large bowl, mix together the pork, beef, breadcrumbs, onion, garlic, oregano, parsley, chilli (if using), egg and seasoning.

Roll the mixture into small balls and place on the lined tray. Bake in a hot oven for 15–18 minutes or brown the meatballs in a large frying pan with some olive oil.

Once the meatballs have cooked, put them in a large saucepan with the tomato sauce. Simmer for 20–30 minutes—you want a thick sauce so your buns don't go soggy.

Split the rolls in half lengthwise and toast them. Line the insides with the sliced provolone cheese, add three meatballs to each roller, top with extra cheese and place the filled rollers back on the baking tray. Place back in the oven until the cheese has melted and the rolls are slightly browned.

Serve with Oven-baked Onion Rings.

Chicken-fried steak rollers

2 lb 4 oz/1 kg round steaks
1 teaspoon salt
1 teaspoon pepper
1 cup all-purpose/plain flour
salt and pepper
2 eggs
1 cup milk

3 tablespoons olive oil
12 roller buns of your choice
mayonnaise
lettuce
tomato, sliced

Cut the steaks to fit the slider buns then tenderise them with a meat mallet or the back of a knife. Season the steaks on both sides with the salt and pepper.

Pour the flour into a wide, shallow dish and season the flour with salt and pepper.

In a separate shallow dish, beat the eggs and milk together. Coat the steaks on both sides in the flour and shake off any excess. Dip the coated steaks into the egg milk mix, coating well, then dip back into the flour. Set aside on a clean plate until all the steaks are coated.

Heat a large non-stick frying pan over a medium-high heat and add enough oil to cover the bottom. Cook the steaks in batches, until golden brown, approximately 3 to 4 minutes per side. Once cooked, set the steaks aside on a plate and keep in a warm oven. Repeat until all the steaks are done.

To assemble your rollers, slice the buns in half lengthways, not slicing all the way through. Spread the opening of the bun with mayonnaise. Add a piece of steak, then some lettuce, a slice of tomato. Hold together with a cocktail stick.

Serve with Beer-battered Fries.

Chicken Banh-Mi rollers

¼ cup rice vinegar
2 teaspoons lime juice
1 teaspoon soy sauce
1 teaspoon fish sauce
½ teaspoon pepper
1 teaspoon sugar
2 large carrots, julienned (thinly sliced)
1 Lebanese cucumber

12 roller buns of your choice
mayonnaise
½ cup fresh cilantro/coriander
1½ cups cooked roast chicken, cooled and shredded
1–2 jalapenos, thinly sliced
soy sauce, to serve

Whisk together the vinegar, lime juice, soy sauce, fish sauce, pepper and sugar in a bowl. Toss through the julienned carrot and allow to marinate for at least 30 minutes.

Using a vegetable peeler or a mandolin, thinly peel the cucumber.

Split a roller bun in half lengthways. Spread the insides with mayonnaise then add cilantro, cucumber, carrot, chicken, a few slices of jalapenos and a sprinkle of soy sauce.

Serve with Asian-style Coleslaw on the side.

chicken and bacon rollers

3 skinless chicken breasts
salt and pepper to taste
1 teaspoon olive oil
12 slices streaky bacon, cut in half

ranch dressing or Blue Cheese Mayonnaise (see
   recipe), to serve
6 slices Swiss cheese, cut in half

Season the chicken with salt and pepper. In a large non-stick frying pan, add 1 teaspoon of oil and cook the chicken for 7–8 minutes each side or until cooked.

In the same pan, cook the bacon until crispy. Remove from the pan and allow to drain on some paper towel. Dice the chicken and bacon, mix together in a bowl and set aside.

Split a roller bun in half lengthways. Spread the inside of the rollers with ranch dressing or Blue Cheese Mayonnaise, add the chicken and bacon mixture and top each roll with a slice of cheese. Place the rollers under a hot broiler or grill until the cheese melts. Thread a cocktail stick through the middle, to keep it together while serving.

Serve with potato chips.

Chicken Fajita roller

3 tablespoons olive oil

juice of half a lemon

1 teaspoon soy sauce

½ teaspoon cumin

½ teaspoon dried oregano

½ teaspoon chilli powder

½ teaspoon paprika

pepper, to taste

2 skinless chicken breast, sliced into strips

½ red/Spanish onion, diced

1 small bell pepper/capsicum, finely diced

12 roller buns of your choice

½ cup tomato salsa

1 cup Guacamole (see recipe)

½ cup sour cream

½ cup cheddar cheese, grated (optional)

In a sealable plastic bag combine 2 tablespoons oil, lemon juice, soy sauce and the spices. Add the chicken strips, seal the bag and leave to marinate in the refrigerator for 1 to 4 hours.

In a large non-stick frying pan, add 1 tablespoon of oil and cook the onions and peppers over a medium-high heat until softened. Remove and set aside.

In the same frying pan, cook the chicken strips for 5–6 minutes. Add the reserved onion and peppers mixture and cook for a further 2 minutes.

Slice the roller buns in half lengthwise and divide the chicken strips between the rollers. Top each roller with salsa, guacamole and sour cream. Sprinkle with cheese if you like. Serve with the hot sauce of your choice.

To make an easy vegetarian slider, simply substitute the chicken with about 12 oz/350 g of tofu.

Beef Sausage and Caramelized Onion rollers

8 beef sausages, linked
I tablespoon butter
I large onion, halved then sliced
salt and pepper, to taste

I teaspoon olive oil
Dijon or yellow mustard, to serve
chives, for garnish (optional)

Keeping the sausages linked, twist them in half to make two smaller sausages (16 in total) and then cut the links.

Heat a frying pan on a medium heat and melt the butter. Add oil and the onion, and cook until golden. Season to taste and set aside to use later.

In the same frying pan, heat the oil and cook the sausages to your liking. When sausages are cooked, split the roller buns in half lengthwise. Toast the rollers, if you like, then add the sausage to the roller bun and top with the onion and mustard. Sprinkle with chives just before serving.

Serve with The Best Potato Salad. For a vegetarian option, try storebought vegetarian sausages. Just cook the sausages first before cutting in half to fit the roller buns.

chicken sausage rollers

8 chicken sausages, linked
I large onion, finely sliced
I large bell pepper/capsicum, finely sliced
I tablespoon butter
I teaspoon olive oil

12 roller buns of your choice
I cup lettuce, sliced
Dijon mustard (optional hot English), to serve

Twist the sausages in half to make two smaller sausages from each sausage and cut at the twist.

Heat the butter in a frying pan over a medium heat. Once the butter is bubbling, cook the onion and pepper until golden. Set aside.

In the same frying pan, heat the oil and cook the sausages until cooked through.

Slice the roller buns in half lengthways and lightly toast the rolls.

Place some lettuce inside each toasted roll. Place a sausage on top, then add some cooked onion and peppers. Serve with Dijon mustard on the side.

If you like some heat, serve these rollers with some Spicy Tomato Sauce on the side.

chipolata wrapped in prosciutto Rollers

12 chipolata or cocktail sausages
12 thin slices prosciutto
I teaspoon olive oil

I tablespoon butter
Tomato and Chilli Jam (see recipe), to serve

Preheat the oven to 350°F/180°C. Line a roasting tray with baking parchment/paper.

Wrap the sausages in a single slice of prosciutto each. Heat the oil in the frying pan over a medium heat, then add the sausages and cook for 4–5 minutes. Transfer the sausages to the lined baking tray and roast for 20 minutes.

Slice the roller buns in half lengthways. Once the sausages have cooked, add a sausage to each bun and top with some Tomato and Chilli Jam.

Serve these with potato chips or Oven-baked Potato Fries.

Pulled pork rollers

1 cup barbecue sauce
½ cup apple cider
½ cup beef stock
1 tablespoon Worcestershire sauce
1 large onion, diced
2 cloves garlic, crushed

1 teaspoon thyme
1 teaspoon chilli powder
4 lb 6 oz/2 kg pork shoulder
20-24 roller buns
Sweet Coleslaw (see recipe), to serve

Combine all the ingredients except for the pork, buns and coleslaw in a bowl and stir. Pour half the sauce into a slow cooker, add the pork, then cover with the rest of the sauce.

Cook, covered, on high heat for 5-6 hours or on low heat for 10 hours. Remove the meat from the slow cooker and pour the sauce into a small saucepan. Bring the sauce to the boil and reduce it until it thickens.

Meanwhile, remove the bone from the pork and, using two forks, shred the meat. Put the meat and the thickened sauce back in the slow cooker to keep warm.

Slice part-way through the buns lengthwise. To assemble the rollers, spoon in enough pork and sauce to fill it.

These rollers are great with Sweet Coleslaw, either on top or as a side.

Alaskan King crab roller

17½ oz/500 g cooked Alaskan king crab, chopped
1 stalk celery, finely chopped
2 tablespoons mayonnaise
2 teaspoons Dijon mustard
1 tablespoon capers, chopped

1 tablespoon lemon juice
salt and pepper
12 roller buns of your choice
butter
watercress, to serve

In a bowl, combine crab, celery, mayonnaise, mustard, capers, lemon juice, and salt and pepper to taste. Refrigerate until ready to use.

Then slice the rollers part-way, spread with some butter and toast under a grill or in the oven on a medium heat. It won't take long to toast them, so keep an eye on them if you don't want them to burn.

Fill up the toasted roller buns with crab mixture and top with watercress.

Fish and mayo rollers

1 tablespoon butter

1 tablespoon oil

1 large fillet of firm, white-fleshed fish,
  pan-fried

½ cup full-fat mayonnaise

1 small red/Spanish onion, finely diced

1½ teaspoon fresh dill

juice of a lemon or lime

salt and pepper, to taste

1 tablespoon capers, chopped

In a large, non-stick frying pan on medium-high heat, heat the butter and oil together.

Once the butter has melted, place in the fish fillet and cook until the fillet turns opaque and starts to flake easily. Make sure the fish is cooked completely before removing from the heat.

In a bowl, mix together the cooked fish flakes, mayonnaise, onion, dill and lemon or lime juice. Once combined, season with salt and pepper. Refrigerate fish mixture until ready to use.

To assemble your rollers, slice the buns part-way lengthwise, add a few tablespoons of the fish mixture and sprinkle some capers over the top.

crab and mayo rollers

17½ oz/500 g cooked crab meat
½ cup full-fat mayonnaise
½ cup sour cream
1 small red/Spanish onion, finely diced
1½ teaspoons fresh dill (or ½ teaspoon dried dill)

juice of half a lemon
salt and pepper, to taste
12 roller buns of your choice
½ cup watercress
1–2 lemons, cut into wedges

In a bowl, combine the crab, mayonnaise, sour cream, onion, dill and lemon juice and mix together. Season with salt and pepper to taste, then cover and refrigerate for an hour before use.

To assemble your rollers, slice the buns part-way through lengthwise and spread the crab mixture into a bun and top with watercress.

Serve with lemon wedges and Qick Tomato Salsa.

Lobster Rollers

17½ oz/500 g cooked lobster or crayfish,
  chopped
I stalk celery, finely chopped
2 tablespoons mayonnaise
2 teaspoons Dijon mustard
I tablespoon capers, chopped

I tablespoon lemon juice
salt and pepper
12–14 roller buns of your choice
butter
watercress or cilantro/coriander, to serve

In a bowl, combine lobster, celery, mayonnaise, mustard, capers, lemon juice, and salt and pepper to taste. Refrigerate until ready to use.

Slice the rollers part-way through and toast it under a grill or in the oven. Then butter the inside and fill with lobster mixture. Top with watercress or cilantro.

Plate them, then warm them in the oven just before serving.

tuna and mayonnaise rollers

1 x 15 oz/425 g can tuna in water, drained
1 cup mayonnaise
1 onion, diced
1 tablespoon capers, finely diced

1 cup cheese, grated
salt and pepper, to taste
dill, to serve

In a bowl, combine the tuna, mayo, onion and capers, and season to taste. Refrigerate until ready to use.

Preheat the oven to 400°F/200°C. To assemble your rollers, slice the roller buns part-way through lengthwise, add the tuna mix and top with cheese. Place on a baking tray and bake in the oven until the cheese has melted. Sprinkle with some dill just before serving and place cocktail skewers through the middle to hold them together.

Serve with a side of Barley, Feta and Pear Salad.

Tofu Rollers

17½ oz/500 g firm tofu
2 tablespoon olive oil
2 clove garlic, crushed
4 teaspoons ground cumin
salt and pepper

4 tablespoons hummus
2 cups mixed salad leaves
1 red bell pepper/capsicum, finely chopped
12 slider buns of your choice

Cut tofu into 12 even slices.

Combine oil, garlic, cumin and seasoning in a bowl. Dip tofu slices in the mix and coat well. Pan-fry the tofu until heated through, about 2 minutes each side.

To assemble the rollers, slice the buns in half and spread one half with some hummus. Add the cooked tofu, the mixed salad leaves and some bell pepper to each bun. Place the other half of the bun on top and hold it together with a cocktail stick.

Spice these up with some chilli sauce or Wasabi Mayonnaise.

sauces, sides and treats

spicy Tomato sauce

½ tablespoon olive oil
1 small onion, finely chopped
1 clove garlic, crushed
1 fresh red chilli, deseeded and finely chopped

1 green bell pepper/capsicum, finely chopped
14 oz/400 g canned crushed tomatoes
pepper

Heat oil in a saucepan and cook onion, garlic, chilli and bell pepper for 5 minutes or until onion and capsicum are soft. Add tomatoes, bring mixture to the boil, then reduce heat and simmer for 15–20 minutes or until sauce thickens. Season to taste with black pepper.

Tomato and chilli jam salsa

2 tablespoons olive oil
1 red/Spanish onion, finely chopped
2 cloves garlic, finely chopped
1 large red chilli, finely chopped
14 oz/400 g chopped tomatoes

10 sun-dried tomatoes, finely chopped
½ cup brown sugar
2 tablespoons balsamic vinegar
salt and freshly ground black pepper

Heat the olive oil in a pan, add the onion, garlic and chilli and cook for about five minutes, until onions are softened.

Tip in the chopped and sun-dried tomatoes and cook over a medium heat for about 10 minutes. Add the sugar and vinegar and bring to a boil, stirring every now and then.

Reduce the heat. While the mixture is reducing, season to taste. The jam is ready when it looks thick.

You can bottle the jam in sterilised containers.

Asian-style coleslaw

1 red cabbage, finely shredded
2 carrots, julienned (thinly sliced)
¼ cup fresh mint, chopped
1 onion, finely sliced

DRESSING
1 tablespoon hot chilli sauce (sriracha is my
    preference)

2 tablespoons fish sauce
2 tablespoons rice wine vinegar
2 tablespoons lime juice
2 tablespoons vegetable oil
2 tablespoons sugar
2 cloves garlic, minced
½ teaspoon ground black pepper

In a large bowl, combine the cabbage, carrot and mint.

In a separate bowl, mix together the onion and dressing ingredients. Pour the dressing over the coleslaw and coat well. Refrigerate until required.

Add some peeled, julienned cucumber if you like.

oven-baked onion rings

olive oil cooking spray
2–3 large onions
¾ cup self-rising/self-raising flour

2 eggs
2 cups fine dried breadcrumbs
1 teaspoon Cajun seasoning

Preheat the oven to 440°F/225°C. Line two large baking trays with baking parchment/paper. Grease the paper with some olive oil spray.

Peel and slice the onions ½ in/1 cm wide. Separate the rings, removing the very small rings from the centre of the onion. You can freeze these for another time or use in another dish. Put the larger rings in a bowl of cold water.

Pour the flour into a shallow dish. Break the eggs into another dish and lightly beat. Mix the breadcrumbs and Cajun seasoning in a bowl. Remove the onion rings, one at a time and drain on some paper towel. Coat each ring in flour, dip the ring in the egg, then coat in the breadcrumb mix, shaking off any excess crumbs. Place the crumbed rings on the lined baking trays.

When all the onion rings are coated and on the trays, spray the onion rings with the oil and bake for about 16–20 minutes. Turn after 8–10 minutes to brown both sides. Cook until golden brown and crispy. Once cooked, remove from oven and place all the onions in a large bowl and salt to taste.

Always make double the quantity of these as they are addictive!

Beer-battered Fries

6 large Pontiac potatoes, cut into thick slices
2 cups all-purpose/plain flour
½ teaspoon baking powder
½ teaspoon salt

13 fl oz/375 ml cold beer
vegetable oil, to deep fry

In a large saucepan of water, par-boil the potato wedges until just cooked through. Set aside to drain and cool. Pat dry with kitchen towel.

In a bowl, mix together 1½ cups of flour, baking powder and salt. Slowly add the beer, a little at a time, whisking into a thin batter.

Coat the cooled wedges in the remaining flour and then dip in the batter. If you have a deep-fryer, fill it to 3 in/7.5 cm with oil. Heat the oil to 350°F/180°C and then cook the potatoes in batches until they are golden brown and cripsy.

If you don't have a kitchen thermometer or deep-fryer, heat up the oil in a large, high-sided saucepan. To test that the oil is hot enough, drop a potato wedge into the oil. If the oil bubbles, it is hot enough to start cooking your fries. Fry the wedges in batches until golden brown and crisp. Keep the fries warm in a low oven, until they are all cooked. Season with salt.

Use a bigger bottle of beer—then you can drink what's left over.

south American bean salad

1½ lb/800 g cans cannellini beans, drained and rinsed

1 small red/Spanish onion, thinly sliced

1 small red bell pepper/capsicum, roasted and thinly sliced

1 jalapeno chilli, deseeded and diced

3 cups watercress sprigs, washed

¼ cup flat-leaf parsley leaves

2 tablespoon extra virgin olive oil

1 tablespoon lemon juice

2 tablespoons red wine vinegar

½ teaspoon sugar

salt and black pepper

Place beans in a serving bowl. Add red onion, roasted bell pepper (see below), jalapeno, watercress and parsley.

Combine olive oil, lemon juice, red wine vinegar, sugar, salt and pepper in a small bowl.

Pour dressing over the bean mixture and toss to combine.

To roast bell pepper, cut into quarters, remove seeds and place under a hot grill for 6–8 minutes or until the skin blackens. Remove skin and thinly slice.

Barley, feta and pear salad

1 cup pearl barley
½ cup walnuts
1 cup fresh flat-leaf parsley leaves
3 stalks celery
1–2 firm ripe pears

3½ oz/100 g fresh arugula/rocket leaves
3½ oz/100 g crumbled feta
juice of 1 lemon
3 tablespoons extra virgin olive oil
salt and pepper

Place the barley in a large saucepan, partially cover with hot water and boil until tender, about 30 minutes.

While barley is cooking, toast walnuts in a small frying pan until golden and fragrant. Set aside. Chop the parsley and cut celery into fine slices. Peel and core pear and cut into fine wedges, then mix with the rocket, parsley and celery.

Drain barley in a sieve and transfer to a bowl. Add feta and nuts and mix well. Add the rocket mixture. Whisk the lemon juice, oil, salt and pepper then toss through salad until combined.

warm herbed potato salad

3 lb/ 1¹/₃ kg russet or Idaho potatoes
2 tablespoons olive oil
¼ cup fresh dill, chopped
¼ cup fresh chervil, chopped
¼ cup fresh parsley, chopped
zest of 1 lemon
salt and pepper
1 serve Caramelised Onions (see recipe)

DRESSING
²/₃ cup olive oil
¹/₃ cup white wine vinegar
juice of 1 lemon
3 cloves garlic

Cut the unpeeled and well-washed potatoes into large chunks and boil in salted water for 10 minutes or until tender but not soft.

Drain the potatoes and return to the saucepan.

In a jug, whisk the dressing ingredients until thickened. Pour the dressing over the hot potatoes and toss, adding the fresh herbs and lemon zest with salt and lots of pepper to taste.

Add the caramelised onions and toss thoroughly.

Tomato and onion Salad With Feta Dressing

4 large tomatoes, thinly sliced
I red/Spanish onion, thinly sliced
salt and pepper, to taste
¼ cup fresh basil, chopped

DRESSING
2½ oz/75 g feta, crumbled
3 tablespoons natural yoghurt
2 tablespoons extra virgin olive oil
I tablespoon white wine vinegar

Arrange the tomato and onion slices on a large serving plate and season with salt and pepper.

In a food processor, or using a hand blender, blend the feta, yoghurt, oil and vinegar until smooth.

Drizzle the dressing over the tomatoes, then sprinkle with basil.

Baby spinach, toasted pine nut and avocado salad

3 oz/90 g capacollo/capicola or prosciutto, sliced
7 oz/ 200 g baby spinach
2 oz/60 g pine nuts, toasted
1 avocado, sliced
¼ cup olive oil

2 tablespoons balsamic vinegar
2 oz/60 g pecorino cheese, shaved
pinch of sea salt
pepper

Place the capacollo under a hot grill and cook until crispy. Place capacollo, spinach, pine nuts and avocado in a bowl.

Mix together the oil and balsamic vinegar, pour over the salad, and then toss through the pecorino shavings.

Season with salt and pepper and serve.

Greek Salad

2 Lebanese cucumbers, sliced

4 Roma tomatoes, quartered

2 red onions, quartered

2½ oz/75g feta, crumbled

½ cup whole Kalamata olives, left whole

3 tablespoons extra virgin olive oil

2 tablespoons brown vinegar

pinch of sea salt

pepper

¼ cup oregano leaves

Place the cucumber, tomatoes, onion, feta and olives in a bowl.

Combine olive oil and vinegar in a separate bowl, and whisk. Pour over the salad, then season with salt and pepper.

Garnish with oregano leaves. Serve salad on its own, or with fresh bread.

caramelized onions

1–2 tablespoons butter
3 large onions, halved and sliced
salt, to taste

1 tablespoon brown sugar
1–2 teaspoons balsamic vinegar

Melt the butter in a frying pan over a low heat. Add the onions and salt and cook slowly until the onions are soft and golden brown, stirring occasionally so they do not catch on the bottom of the pan.

Add the sugar and the vinegar. Cook for a further 10 minutes stirring occasionally until sticky and brown.

Use immediately or allow to cool and store in a glass or plastic container, in the fridge.

For some variety, add 1 bell pepper/capsicum, thinly sliced, at the same time as the onions. A great side to any slider or roller.

Chilli for rollers

I teaspoon olive oil

I medium white onion, finely diced

2 cloves garlic

3½ oz/100 g bacon, diced

I–2 fresh jalapenos, finely diced (optional, for extra heat)

14 oz/400 g ground/minced beef

I teaspoon chilli powder

I teaspoon paprika

I teaspoon cumin

I x 14 oz/400 g can crushed tomatoes

I teaspoon Worcestershire sauce

I cup beef stock

salt and pepper, to taste

Heat the oil in a large frying pan, over a medium-high heat. Add the finely diced onion and garlic and cook until golden. Add the diced bacon and cook until crispy. Stir in the jalapenos now if you want an extra kick.

Add the ground beef and all the spices. Stir and break up the beef. Once the beef has browned, add the tomatoes, Worcestershire sauce and stock, and bring to the boil. Simmer for 30 minutes or until thickened to your liking.

This can be prepared the day before; just reheat before serving.

oven-baked potato fries

17½ oz/500 g baking potatoes
cooking spray

seasoned salt

Preheat the oven to 440°F/230°C.

Peel and thinly slice the potatoes, using a mandolin, and dry between sheets of paper towel. Line a baking tray with baking parchment/paper and lightly spray with cooking spray. Spread the potatoes out on the tray in a single layer and spray with cooking oil and shake over the seasoned salt.

Bake the potatoes for 20 minutes, turning after 10 minutes, until golden brown and crisp.

Try sweet potatoes instead of potatoes. Use a mandolin to slice the potato thinly but be careful with your fingers.

spicy baked wedges with sour cream dip

1 teaspoon ground cumin

1 teaspoon ground coriander

1 teaspoon chilli powder

1 teaspoon paprika (sweet or hot)

¼ cup olive oil

2lb 4oz/1 kg large potatoes, washed and scrubbed,
   cut into wedges

salt and pepper, to taste

SOUR CREAM DIP

9 fl oz/250 ml sour cream

4 fl oz/125 ml sweet chilli sauce

Preheat the oven to 440°F/225°C. Line a large baking tray with baking parchment/paper.

In a large bowl, whisk together the spices and oil. Toss the wedges in the spiced oil and then arrange on the baking tray in a single layer. Bake for around 40 minutes until golden, turning once.

Once you've removed them from the oven, season to taste. Mix together the sour cream and sweet chilli sauce and serve with the baked wedges.

Why not try sweet potato wedges instead? Or replace the sour cream in the dip with a mashed avocado for a dairy-free alternative.

sweet coleslaw

1 small head cabbage, finely chopped
2 carrots, peeled and grated
1 red/Spanish onion, finely sliced

DRESSING
1 cup whole egg mayonnaise
¼ cup apple cider
3 tablespoons sugar
salt and pepper, to taste

In a large bowl, combine the cabbage, carrot and onion. In a separate bowl, mix together the mayonnaise, cider and sugar and season to taste.

Add the dressing to the cabbage and coat well. Refrigerate until required.

If you have a mandolin, use it to slice the vegetables. It will be quicker and easier.

chinese Hot Mustard

¼ cup dry mustard powder
¼ cup cold water
¼ teaspoon vegetable oil

Mix the mustard powder with the water to form a paste. Add the oil and stir well. Let it sit for about an hour before using.

Don't use as much as with regular mustard as it is quite hot. Store in a small jar in the fridge. It should last about one month.

This is great on hot dogs or burgers with pork or lamb—as long as you like it hot.

garlic mayonnaise

¾ cup whole egg mayonnaise

2 tablespoons Greek yoghurt

I teaspoon lemon juice

I tablespoon parsley, finely chopped

I garlic clove, minced

Whisk the ingredients together in a small bowl. Cover with cling wrap then refrigerate until ready to use.

Pineapple Salsa

I x 8 oz/220 g canned diced pineapple, drained
  or I cup fresh pineapple, diced
I small red/Spanish onion, diced
¼ cup cilantro/coriander, finely chopped

juice of I lime
I red chilli, finely diced (optional)
salt and pepper

In a large bowl, mix together the pineapple, onion and cilantro.

Squeeze in the lime juice, sprinkle with chilli and toss. Season with salt and pepper. Cover and refrigerate until serving.

quick Tomato salsa

4–5 ripe tomatoes, de-seeded and diced
I red/Spanish onion, finely diced
¼ cup fresh cilantro/coriander (or use ¼ cup
parsley)

I teaspoon dried oregano
juice of half a lemon
I tablespoon olive oil
salt and pepper to taste

In a large bowl, toss together the diced tomatoes, onions, cilantro and oregano.

Squeeze the lemon juice over the tomato mix and drizzle with olive oil. Season to taste, toss well and let everything marinate for 10–15 minutes. Cover and refrigerate until serving.

This is a great topping for sliders or rollers. If you like, add some chopped fresh mint or a tablespoon of balsamic vinegar. Or add a finely diced red chilli—leave in the seeds if you like extra heat!

spicy seafood sauce

½ cup mayonnaise (whole egg or Kewpie)
¼ cup ketchup/tomato sauce

1 tablespoon hot sauce (optional)
juice of half a lemon

In a bowl, mix together the mayonnaise, ketchup, hot sauce and lemon juice.

Cover with cling wrap and refrigerate until required.

Just double or halve the quantity as required. Add more hot sauce according to taste.

This sauce will go great on any seafood slider or roller if you want a bit of heat.

Sliders and rollers are great food for every occasion—relaxed weekend drinks with friends, finger food for cocktail parties, picnics and late-night treats.

Tartare sauce

1 cup mayonnaise (whole egg or Kewpie)
2 tablespoons gherkins, finely chopped
2 tablespoons chives, finely chopped
2 tablespoons fresh parsley, finely chopped

1 tablespoon Dijon mustard
juice of half a lemon
salt and pepper to taste

In a small bowl, combine all ingredients. Refrigerate until ready for use.

Halve or double the amount to make less or more.

The Best Potato Salad

3 lb 5 oz/1.5 kg chat potatoes, whole and
  unpeeled
3 rashers bacon, rind and excess fat removed,
  then diced
¾ cup sour cream
½ cup whole egg mayonnaise

1 tablespoon wholegrain mustard
1 large red/Spanish onion, finely diced
1 bunch fresh chives, finely chopped
salt and pepper
hard-boiled eggs, halved (optional)

Put the potatoes in a large saucepan, cover with water and add a teaspoon of salt. Place the saucepan over a medium heat and bring to the boil. Reduce the heat and cook the potatoes until tender.

While potatoes are cooking, cook the bacon in a frying pan, over a medium heat until crispy. Remove from the pan and drain on some paper towel.

Once the potatoes are cooked, drain and set aside until cool to the touch. Quarter the potatoes.

In a large bowl, mix together the sour cream, mayonnaise, wholegrain mustard and onion. Add the potato and bacon and sprinkle with the fresh chives. If you like, top the salad with a few halved boiled eggs.

Use cooking scissors to chop the chives.

Four-bean salad

½ cup dry couscous (I use the instant variety)
½ cup boiling water
I x 14 oz/400 g can four-bean mix
2 large tomatoes, seeded and diced
I cucumber, peeled and diced
I red/Spanish onion, diced
¼ cup parsley (optional)

I large carrot, diced (optional)
2 celery stalks, diced (optional)
salt and pepper to taste

DRESSING
I fl oz/30 ml (more or less)good-quality olive oil
3 tablespoons balsamic vinegar

Put the couscous in a bowl. Pour the boiling water over the couscous and let it sit for 5 minutes or as per the instructions on the packet. Set aside to cool until ready to use.

Drain and rinse the four-bean mix, until the water runs clear. Place bean mix in a large bowl, and add the couscous and all the other salad ingredients. Toss everything together to combine.

Whisk the dressing ingredients together and pour over the salad. Add salt and pepper to taste. Chill in the refrigerator before serving.

Tomato sauce for meatballs

2 tablespoons olive oil
1 small onion, finely diced
1 clove garlic, crushed
1 x 15 oz/440 g can crushed tomatoes
1 teaspoon sugar
1 tablespoon parsley

1 teaspoon oregano
1 teaspoon basil
¼ teaspoon dried chilli flakes (optional)
¼ teaspoon ground black pepper
salt, to taste

In a large saucepan, heat the oil over a low heat. Add the onions and cook for 5 minutes or until soft but not brown.

Add the garlic, cook for another minute, then add the tomato and the rest of the ingredients. Simmer for 20 minutes, stirring occasionally. Set aside to use for the meatballs.

TZatZiki

1 cup thick Greek-style yoghurt

2 garlic cloves, grated

1 Lebanese cucumber, grated and liquid squeezed

2 tablespoons mint leaves, chopped

1 teaspoon olive oil

In a bowl, combine the yoghurt, garlic, cucumber, mint and olive oil. Refrigerate before use.

wasabi mayonnaise

½ cup mayonnaise (whole egg or Kewpie)

1 tablespoon wasabi paste (add more if you like
  it hot)

juice of half a lime

In a bowl, mix together the mayonnaise, wasabi paste and lime juice.

Cover with cling wrap and refrigerate until required.

guacamole

2 ripe avocados
3 tablespoons lemon juice

1 clove garlic, crushed
1 small red onion, finely diced

Cut the avocados lengthwise and discard the stones. Scoop out the flesh with a large spoon and place in a medium bowl.

Add in the lemon juice and garlic. Mash everything together with the back of a fork until fairly smooth. Stir through the onion and transfer to a small serving dish. Cover with cling wrap and chill until ready to serve.

cilantro and Mint Chutney

3 bunches fresh cilantro/coriander, leaves only
1 bunch fresh mint, leaves only
6–8 green chillies
3 teaspoons fresh ginger, finely chopped
6 cloves garlic, finely chopped

2 tablespoons lemon juice
1 tablespoon caster sugar
¼ cup water
salt to taste

Place cilantro, mint, chillies, ginger, garlic, lemon juice, sugar, water and salt in a food processor or blender and process to a paste.

Spoon chutney into a sterilised jar, cover and refrigerate until ready to use.

onion chutney

2 large red/Spanish onions, finely chopped
1¾ oz/50 g brown sugar

1 tablespoon white wine vinegar

Place all the ingredients in a saucepan and bring to the boil over a low heat. Simmer uncovered for about 20 minutes, or until almost all the liquid has evaporated.

Use immediately but can be stored in the refrigerator for about a week.

Blue cheese Mayonnaise

¼ teaspoon dry mustard
2 egg yolks
I cup olive oil

2 tablespoons lemon juice or white wine vinegar
ground pepper
3 oz/90 g blue cheese, crumbled

Place mustard and egg yolks in a food processor or blender and process until just combined. With machine running, gradually pour in oil and process until mixture thickens.

Blend in lemon juice or vinegar and pepper to taste. Add the blue cheese and process to combine.

sweet Chilli yoghurt

1 cup low-fat natural yoghurt
2 tablespoons sweet chilli sauce

1 tablespoon lime juice

To make chilli yoghurt, place yoghurt, chilli sauce and lime juice in a bowl and whisk to combine. Cover and refrigerate until required.

cilantro yoghurt

1 cup Greek-style yoghurt
2 tablespoons cilantro/coriander, chopped

1 tablespoon lemon juice
pepper, to taste

In a bowl, mix together all of the ingredients. Cover and refrigerate until required.

ice cream brioche sliders

1 quart/1 litre tub vanilla ice cream
grated chocolate or Milo chocolate milk powder

12 brioche slider buns

Take the ice cream out of the freezer and leave in the refrigerator to soften a little. Once softened, remove the ice cream from the tub onto a chopping board and slice the block of ice cream into ¾ in/2 cm thick slices.

Using a cookie cutter, cut out 12 discs of ice cream from the thickly cut slices. Place the ice cream discs onto a baking parchment/paper-lined tray and return to the freezer. Place the leftover ice cream back into the plastic tub and return to the freezer.

Once the discs have been frozen again, roll the outside of the ice cream discs in the chocolate.

Slice the brioche buns in half lengthways. Place the ice cream round on the bottom half and place on the top. Serve immediately.

If not serving the sliders immediately, keep the ice cream rounds in the freezer, until ready to serve.

chocolate sliders with chocolate sauce

1 quart/1 litre vanilla ice cream
12 brioche slider buns

CHOCOLATE SAUCE
2½ oz/75 g dark chocolate, chopped
½ cup pure cream
2 tablespoons brown sugar

Take the ice cream out of the freezer and leave in the refrigerator to soften a little. Once softened, remove the ice cream from the tub onto a chopping board and slice the block of ice cream into ¾ in/2 cm thick slices.

Using a cookie cutter, cut out 12 discs of ice cream from the thickly cut slices. Place the ice cream discs onto a baking parchment/paper-lined tray and return to the freezer until ready to use. Place the leftover ice cream back into the plastic tub and return to the freezer.

To make the chocolate sauce, place all the ingredients in a microwave-safe jug and microwave on medium-high for 2–3 minutes, stirring every minute, until the chocolate has melted and the sauce is smooth.

Slice the buns in half lengthways and place an ice cream disc on the bottom bun, top with chocolate sauce then add the top of the bun. Serve immediately.

variations

Chilli chocolate: In a small saucepan, bring the cream almost to the boil over a low heat. Take the cream off the heat and add in two halved chillies and set it aside to infuse for 5–10 minutes. Strain the chilli from the cream then stir in the chocolate and sugar, until the chocolate has melted.

Mocha: Add a teaspoon of coffee granules into the chocolate sauce after the first minute of heating.

Frangelico: Add 2 tablespoons of Frangelico once the sauce is heated and smooth.

vanilla sliders with pecan caramel sauce

4 oz/125 g butter
¾ cup brown sugar
¾ cup cream
I teaspoon vanilla extract

½ cup pecans, chopped
I quart/I litre vanilla ice cream
12 brioche buns

In a small saucepan, melt the butter and sugar over a medium-high heat.

Once the butter has melted and the sugar has dissolved, add the cream. Bring it to a boil and reduce the heat.

Cook for a further 5 minutes until the sauce has thickened. Add the vanilla and pecans and take the sauce off the heat. Let it stand for 5 minutes to cool.

Take the ice cream out of the freezer and leave in the refrigerator to soften a little. Once softened, remove the ice cream from the tub onto a chopping board and slice the block of ice cream into ¾ in/2 cm thick slices.

Using a cookie cutter, cut out 12 discs of ice cream from the thickly cut slices. Place the ice cream discs onto a baking parchment/paper-lined tray and return to the freezer until ready to use. Place the leftover ice cream back into the plastic tub and return to the freezer.

Slice the slider buns in half. Place one ice cream disc on each bun half, drizzle with the slightly cooled sauce, then place on the top bun. Serve immediately.

Acknowledgements

One of the greatest pleasures in life is cooking the food you love for family and friends and over the years I've done my fair share of cooking and entertaining, which has inspired the easy recipes that have come to life in *Sliders and Rollers*.

There are several people to thank who've contributed to this book. Firstly, my twin brother John, the second best cook in my family. Without his help during the photo shoot I wouldn't have made it, even though I had to constantly remind him: 'John, read the recipe!'

To my enthusiastic editor Jodi De Vantier thank you, you made writing a book a joyful experience as did my designers Tracy and Keisha. Also, to the best girl in production, Olga, who can't cook but loves my pork belly sliders—lucky her hubby Terry can cook. Special thanks to the 'unseen' team at New Holland Publishers—Lesley, Tony, Marc, Sacha, the sales guru, and Jackie the general manager of Spank stationery. It might not be stationery, Jackie, but I know you'll love it! The sales teams across the globe, who will be selling my book, thank you.

To my author manager, Patsy 'just half a glass of wine, thanks' Rowe, guru and pocket dynamo, and her ever-patient husband, Dr Bill who eats everything I put in front of him!

To my daughter, Emaleigh, for sharing her recipe with me and to my Mum and Dad, which one of you taught me to cook?

To my very cool, and easy to work with, photographer Sue Stubbs, love your work. Thank you, I know we all worked so hard and I appreciate your support during my first shoot. And to Bhavani, my stylist, we did get there in the end, thank you.

To Fiona Susanto who photographed our people shots, thank you, it was a lot of fun and you were like one of the family within minutes.

Big thank you to a great bunch of friends, Irish John, Mal and Vicki, the fabulous miss Hilary Higgins, Simon and Kelly, Dave and Denise, Brooke and Marcus, Krystan, Max, Paul and Claire Reynolds who have all eaten enough of my cooking for a lifetime—don't worry Claire, I shall teach Sophie to cook.

To my wife, yes I know I talk about food a lot but I'm not hitting my word limit every day.

Above all, thank you to the booksellers for your invaluable support of *Sliders and Rollers*.

Readers, I hope you enjoy this book. What started out as a bit of fun has turned into my passion and has added to my taste tester's waistlines. I hope you'll enjoy not only trying some of these easy recipe ideas for yourself but will introduce your family and friends to *Sliders and Rollers*.

Eat, drink and enjoy!

David Cowie

Recipe Index

First published in 2013 by
New Holland Publishers
London • Cape Town • Sydney • Auckland

www.newhollandpublishers.com

Garfield House 86–88 Edgware Road London W2 2EA United Kingdom
Wembley Square First Floor Solan Road Gardens Cape Town 8001 South Africa
1/66 Gibbes Street Chatswood NSW 2067 Australia
218 Lake Road Northcote Auckland New Zealand

A catalogue record of this book is available at the British Library and at the National Library of Australia.

ISBN: 9781742574028

10 9 8 7 6 5 4 3 2 1

Publisher: Fiona Schultz
Project editor: Jodi De Vantier
Designer: Tracy Loughlin
Stylist: Bhavani Konings
Food Photographer: Sue Stubbs except pages 74, 78, 80, 82, 140, 145, 152, 157, 159, 161, 207 (NHIL).
Event Photographer: Fiona Susanto
Production director: Olga Dementiev
Printer: Toppan Leefung Printing Limited

Follow New Holland Publishers on
Facebook: www.facebook.com/NewHollandPublishers

BT